Such Love

Marjorie Gull

Such Love

A collection of poems.

Copyright ©marjoriegull2016

All rights reserved.
The moral right of the author has been asserted.
No part of this publication may be reproduced, stored in a retrieval system, or transmitted in any form or by any means, without the prior consent of the author, nor be otherwise circulated in any form of binding or cover other than that in which it is published and without a similar condition being imposed on the subsequent purchaser.

British Library Cataloguing in Publication Data.

A CIP catalogue record for this book is available from the British Library.

Acknowledgements

Thank you to Heather Hart for the lovely illustrations

Content	Page
Such Love	7
Such Peace	8
Heaven	9
Such Certainty	11
Such Assurance	13
Such Understanding	14
Such Joy	15
Just For You	16
Misunderstood	17
Such Trust	19
Such Comfort	20
The Greatest Gift	22
Such Power	23
Such Hurt	24

Content	Page
Unconditional Love	26
Simple Heartfelt Prayers	27
Angels	29
Broken Dreams	32
Such Hope	34
Transformed	36

Such Love

I cried to You, Lord,
That I should hear Your
voice divine.
I cried to You, Lord,
That on Your loving breast I might recline.
And as I cried there opened up to me
A scene depicting Calvary…
I looked up to the centre cross –
I saw You hanging there, arms stretched wide,
Bleeding side…
I cried!

Your head bowed down,
Yes…there was a crown – Diamonds? Jewels?
No… Just cruel thorns.
Oh Jesus, such deep love for me,
Shown that day at Calvary.
Love I never can repay,
So, from my heart Lord,
Thank You for that wondrous day.
Thank You Lord for giving me
That precious glimpse of Calvary.

Such Peace

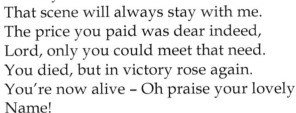

My thoughts returned to Calvary –
That scene will always stay with me.
The price you paid was dear indeed,
Lord, only you could meet that need.
You died, but in victory rose again.
You're now alive – Oh praise your lovely Name!

My heart cries out in Love to You…
I proclaim You Jesus – Lord and King,
My Saviour, You are everything,
And now such peace, as only You can give, is mine.
In return, Lord for You, may I shine.
My heartfelt prayer is all may see –
That Jesus lives and reigns in me.

Heaven

I dreamed I was in Heaven
And, oh the sights I saw.
All around, a sea of faces
Such a vision never witnessed before.

As I gazed at the throng around me,
Expressions of love on each face,
I was struck with awe and wonder
At God's amazing grace.

Looking and listening, I was spellbound.
I heard anthems of worship and praise
Being sung to the God of all ages
By redeemed ones from every race.

As I looked down the streets of Heaven,
And saw they were paved with gold,
The verses in Revelation
Gradually began to unfold.

The river of Life, clear as crystal;
The city itself pure gold;
Heaven's pearly gates wide open;
A wonderful sight to behold.

Seeing round me such perfection
My thoughts were constantly turned
To the One who Himself was perfect,
Whom the world had so sadly spurned.

As I stood enthralled and listening
I felt such joy in my heart.
I heard God's choir ever singing –
'My God, how great thou art'.

From my dream, I then awakened,
So thankful, one day, I will be
In Heaven, at home with my Saviour,
Whose face I am longing to see.

Will you, one day, enter Heaven
And hear God say, "Welcome home"?
You may, by confessing Jesus as Lord –
Who is God's eternal Son.

Such Certainty

How secure do you feel at the
end of the day?
Do you have full assurance, if you kneel and
Pray,
That the One who has founded the great
Universe
Will, himself in the future, all evil reverse?
We hear, now, every day of much sorrow and
Pain.
Of lives torn apart again and again.
And best chosen remedies, all proving in vain.
Do you dream of a day when all will be
Peace?
No warring factions, hostilities all cease.
No longer the heartaches, sorrow and crying,
And fears at last gone, no more sickness or
Dying.
Then take comfort in listening to words Jesus
spoke,
With authority no alien power can revoke.

> *'God shall wipe away all tears.*
> *No more death, no more fears.*

Never again any crying or pain' (i)

This promise, the Bible itself makes so plain,
Is effective for those who believe in His name.
And this is no dream, Yes this is for real.

Jesus, one day, is coming again. (ii)

Then questions arise; where shall I stand,
How shall I feel
Perhaps you've not thought about Christ's Return,
Or even considered it your concern.
Reading these words calls for response.
May your cry be today –
Lord show me the way.

                        (i) Revelation Ch.21 v.4
                        (ii) John Ch.14 vv.1-4

Such Assurance

The name of Jesus is so dear,
In Him I know there is no fear.
Each circumstance of life I see
His guiding hand is leading me,
When doubts crowd in I hear Him say…
Just trust my child, for I'm the way.
Then trusting, keeping close to Me,
Your hand in mine, you then will see
How precious is your life to Me,
The peace, the happiness I give
Is yours as long as you shall live.

Soon with what joy, Your face I'll see –
Which was so marred at Calvary.
And now with love, looks down on me.

All barriers gone! I now am free
To praise the One who died for me.

Such Understanding

A longing and yearning for time
set apart,
To tell You, Lord Jesus, just what's in my
Heart.
I plan and arrange, as most of us do,
Then find that things happen to rob me of
You.
I attempt once again, but try as I may
I find time has gone – it's the end of the day!

Often in life, Lord, I have such a day,
When I find it impossible even to pray
In times such as these, just keep me aware
Of Your infinite love, understanding and care.
Still for me, Lord Jesus, most precious of all
Is knowing You're there whenever I call.

Such Joy

There's a love in my heart,
Lord, for You,
A love You've made
wonderfully true.
When I think of Your love,
Your compassion and care
I feel I must always, Your beauty declare.

I wake up each morning – another new day,
'We'll face this together' I hear my Lord say
And as the day passes, the highs and the lows,
Through happiness, heartache, still Your love glows.

Evening approaches – the day's at an end…
Such Joy knowing Jesus as Saviour and Friend.

Just For You

I woke up this morning with you
on my Mind.
On gathering my thoughts: I was only to find
Your face that appeared then so clearly in
View
Showed hurt, pain and anguish –
bewilderment too.
It seemed to me that your whole heart was
Laid bare,
Exposing such sadness and seeming despair.
You so touched my heart that I wanted to say,
Don't fret, my dear one, give to Jesus today
Those burdens which on you so heavily lay…
But sadly your heart is so heavy with grief,
To pray isn't easy, so finding relief.
Today, then, my dear one, a prayer just for
You
That Jesus Himself will still carry you
Through,
And that you'll find in Him such a precious
Release,
And for each new day a real sense of His
Peace.

Misunderstood

Misunderstandings – who
 hasn't been that way
  A chance remark,
   misunderstood, can cloud a happy day
    How Satan, in his subtlety,
     Seeks to rob us of our joy
    By planting seeds of doubt and fear
     Remember – it's his ploy
    Then, satisfied he's spoilt our day
    He swiftly turns and walks away
Now Satan before you craftily walk away
  And smugly think you've won the day
  There are certain things, before you go,
    I really think you ought to know:
    Jesus Christ is my dearest friend
    It is on Him that I depend
   He constantly shows His love for me
And channels my thinking to how it should be
    Desiring, always, what is best for me.

But Satan, your quest in life is to misrepresent
  With distortion, lies and evil intent
 How many times do we think wrong thoughts
   And finish up feeling sad and distraught?

When in doubt and querying something that's said
And conflicting thoughts dart through your head
Don't allow Satan to twist and distort
Ask Jesus to redefine those thoughts.

Such Trust

'Please Mummy let me hold
Your hand',
We've often heard it said.
A simple, childlike gesture
Does away with fear and dread.
To trust someone and know that trust won't
ever be betrayed,
Is something very precious
...cannot always be repaid.

How hard it is sometimes,
Just who and when to trust.
Yet life requires at certain times,
A feeling – yes, we must.

So trust we do implicitly
Then find to our dismay,
That trust is made a mockery of
The very following day.

There's someone I can always trust,
A never failing friend.
Who loves me, keeps me, guides me,
Through to my journey's end.
In every way I find Him true.
Will YOU then trust and prove Him too?
His name is Jesus.

Such Comfort

Have you sat at the bedside
Of one you hold so dear?
Wondering what tomorrow brings
Just fills your heart with fear.

As you watch and feel so helpless
Longing thoughts just fill your mind.
If only you could change things –
Leave all this grief behind.

Your heart cries out in anguish
As you know things are the same.
The miracle you prayed for
Hasn't happened – who's to blame?

Your mind in utter turmoil
You're constantly reasoning why.
You sense dark clouds are gathering
To blacken out your sky.

In tenderness, let me point you
To the One who sees you cry.
With His love and His compassion
He'll wipe each tear from your eye.

Jesus knows your every heartache
And longs to comfort you.
Reach out to Him in your sadness
You'll find Him loving, kind and true.

The Greatest Gift

With Christmas fast approaching,
Out comes the Christmas tree.
I'd like to give them oh, so much
Those that are dear to me.

The gifts that I would want for them
Money cannot buy.
You wouldn't find them on a tree
However hard you try.
These gifts are priceless treasures
For they mean so much to all.
The largest gift-wrapped parcel
Couldn't match….however tall.

The gifts I, then desire for them
Are tokens of my love they are:
To be loved, to be healthy
To be happy – no need to be wealthy
To have peace – important to living.
Show compassion, generous in giving.

My heartfelt wish in possessing these gifts
Their lives more enriched will be.
But to head my list is the Greatest Gift –
The love of God's dear Son.
My prayer for them is simple –
To experience and accept
Receiving all the gifts in one.

Such Power

Is your life with power assisted?
Who controls your steering wheel?
Do "you" make all the hard decisions?
Is life all just one big deal?
What about life's many pressures,
Do you find them hard to bear?
How about that inner turmoil,
Things you cannot always share.
Do you know "God's" love and power –
It is constant, without end.
All life's problems he can manage
Even broken hearts will mend.

Choosing a God assisted life,
His power will be applied.
The Holy Spirit He will send.
His peace He will provide.
When Jesus comes into our hearts,
We can on Him depend.
And oh, the joy of knowing
He's our forever friend.

Such Hurt

What happened to rob me
Of the joy that once I had?
Now each day something happens
Which tends to make me sad.

I need Your arms around me Lord,
To feel your face near mine.
To know Your all-embracing love
I then will feel just fine.

Life's hurts and disappointments
Seem all too hard to bear.
Just love me Lord and help me
Take each hurt to You in prayer.

Then as I look to You Lord
Each hurt will seem so small.
I shall thank You then for being
My absolute all-in-all.

And thank You Lord for listening
How you let me hear Your voice.
Always telling me how much You care
Just makes my heart rejoice.
Your peace, now, Lord is in my heart
And You've promised it will stay.

Your love will ever hold me fast
As I approach the day.
Assured You'll intercede for me
In each and every way.

Unconditional Love

Do you need someone to love you?
Someone who you know will care.
Perhaps you feel your life is empty
Seems no-one with whom to share.

Do you often dread tomorrow
Long before today is through.
Do you long to have a friend –
Someone loyal, someone true.
If you're feeling sad and lonely
And you yearn for lasting love…

Do you know my precious Saviour,
Jesus Christ, the Son of God –
He has changed my life completely
Loves and cares so much for me.

Love He fully demonstrated,
When He died at Calvary
For the wrongs that I've committed,
He bore the guilt instead of me.
Our response is in accepting,
This He so desires to see.
So no longer be despondent.
Trust His love – completely free.
Know the peace He will provide.
As your loving friend and guide.

Simple Heartfelt Prayers

Our prayers need not be eloquent or hard to understand
Just something simple from the heart, not anything you've planned.

I find, sometimes, I simply pray and thank the Lord above
For daily blessings He bestows and His unfailing love.

And then, perhaps, it may be just a prayer for someone dear
Or a friend who seems confused and sad, whose life is full of fear.

Another time we need to pray is on behalf of one
Whose life has been turned upside-down, enduring cloud not sun.

For such a one, with loving hearts, we pray a special prayer
That they may feel God's precious love, His tenderness to share.

Then there are those, who sadly, through sickness cannot pray
They feel so weak and helpless as they cling to each new day.

Their strength comes then from you and me, who intercede and pray
That the love and peace of Jesus will surround them, come what may.

So, all in all, dear praying one, never cease to pray.

For heartfelt prayer offered up – God never turns away
We will never know the wealth of prayer until that coming day.

Angels

A Mother's intercessory prayer
Saved her son from his worst nightmare…
Angels surrounded him.

A child at risk of being abused
Remains unscathed, in no way confused…
Angel's surrounded her.

A schoolboy's life miraculously saved
Thankful parents – God's promise
portrayed…
Angels surrounded him.

A four-wheel drive out of control
Driver emerged – dazed but whole…
Angels surrounded him.

A drug addict poised to take his life
Wondrously restrained, then restored to his wife…
Angels surrounded him.

A housewife could have been so badly burned
Not a blemish, again God's promise confirmed …
Angels surrounded her.

Ministering Angels – guiding and protecting night and day
These are mere coincidences some would even say.

But if you read Psalm 91 verse 11*
You'll find a wonderful promise from God in
Heaven.

Guardian and Protecting Angels of whom we're
unaware
Are, again, God's proof of his tender, loving care.

You may not have realised until today
What part in our lives the Angels can play.

Did you ask, 'Angels, surround my child today?'
Or for a loved one living far away.

'He will give His Angels charge over you
To keep you from all harm'*
Some comforting words leave a heart at peace
So assured and inwardly calm.
(These are true incidents.)

Broken Dreams

Broken dreams – lives lay shattered
High hopes gone of things that mattered.
A longed-for baby came, but sadly didn't stay
Now all the aspirations have simply gone
away.
Loving arms now feel rejected
A nursery – so fondly prepared.
All these things and more beside
To show how much we cared.

Now sad and disappointed
Our lives seem hard to bear.
Lord Jesus, in your tenderness
Love and show us how you care.

Gentle Shepherd for the future
Our strength and hope to face each day.
And the confidence in knowing
You're there beside us all the way.

My dear child, I love you
I will never stop loving you.
I've felt your grief, seen you cry
And shared with you those bitter tears.
I've seen your mind in utter turmoil
And longed to quieten all your fears.

I love you and so want to comfort you.
Will you speak to Me – tell Me all your heartaches??
Will you respond to My love, trust Me
And prove I am the One on whom you can depend.
I am Jesus, your Forever Friend.

Psalm 34, v18
> The Lord is close to the broken hearted
> He saves those who have lost all hope.

Zephaniah 3, v17
> The Lord your God is with you
> His power gives you strength
> The Lord will take delight in You
> And in his love give you new hope.

Such Hope

I awoke one morning to find just
blackness –
Not greyness –grey is a colour of hope.
This was blackness, portraying no hope.
Sadly, I asked myself, how shall I ever cope?
My heart is crying out, my soul despairs,
So much doubt, the feeling – nobody cares.
Grief just overwhelmed me.

I sat, just staring into space,
When suddenly I saw His face –
The face of Jesus, oh, so dear,
Then His words came loud and clear:
'I will not leave you comfortless,
I will come to you'.
My agonised response was, 'Come Lord,
Heal my aching heart,
And help me still do my part'.

Sitting quietly I saw, heard and felt the
Immensity of God's love: the gentle touch of
Jesus, whose understanding, tenderness and
Compassion washed over me as a flowing
River.
It was then the healing process began –
At first painful, then, with Jesus at my side,

The hurting cushioned in His love, I was able
Gradually to face each new day with serenity
And peace.

******

Now resting in that love the blackness is fading,
to be replaced by such hope found only
in the One who turns darkness into light:
My precious Saviour, the Lord Jesus Christ.

Transformed

Life: Does it seem, at the moment, an uphill climb?
Or is it peaceful, happy, completely sublime?
We know after sunshine – often comes rain.
But as in life, after happiness – often comes pain.
One day all this will change, I'll explain to you why:
For those trusting Jesus, He'll appear in the sky.
We'll be caught up to join Him, in the twinkling of an eye. *
Then *transformed* to His likeness, redeemed we shall stand.
We shall then enter fully into all God has planned.
There will be no more heartache, sickness or crying
No more pain or suffering, fear or dying…**

At home in God's Heaven – what joy it will be.
With Jesus, our Saviour, whose face we shall see
And loved ones to greet us, what a day that will be.
Won't it be wonderful there!

*1 Corinthians vv52, 53
**Revelation 21 v4

Dear Reader

If you have enjoyed reading this book, then please leave a review on Amazon.

Thank you.

About The Author

Marjorie is a loving wife and mother who spends her time taking care of her husband and her home. She has been an inspiration to those who know her and has the gift of being able to love all she meets, although now in her twilight years she has a passion for GOD's word and continues to trust him through good and bad times.

She is happy that she can now share her poems with you all and pray you will get the same sense of love and peace reading them as she did when she wrote them.

Printed in Great Britain
by Amazon